EARTH SCIENCE LIBRARY

THE OCEANS

MARTYN BRAMWELL

Updated Edition

Franklin Watts

New York · Chicago · London · Toronto · Sydney

Jov.
GC21.5. B73 1994

Second Edition
© 1987, 1994 by
Franklin Watts
All rights reserved

Franklin Watts
95 Madison Avenue
New York, NY 10016

Library of Congress
Cataloging-in-Publication Data

Bramwell, Martyn.
The oceans / by Martyn Bramwell. –
Rev. ed.
p. cm. – (Earth science library)
Includes index.
ISBN 0–531–14304–X
1. Ocean – Juvenile literature. 2. Marine
biology – Juvenile literature. [1. Ocean.]
I. Title. II. Series: Bramwell, Martyn.
Earth science library.
GC21.5.B73 1994
551.46 — dc20   93–40312
                                CIP   AC

Printed in Belgium

Designed by Ben White

Picture research by Mick
Alexander

Illustrations:
Chris Forsey
Hayward Art Group
Colin Newman/Linden Artists

Photographs:
J Allan Cash 12*r*
Ardea 8*r*
Bruce Coleman 13, 22*l*
Robert Estall 16
Robert Harding 21, 22*r*, 28
Frank Lane 29*l*
NASA 5
Seaphot 1, 4, 8*l*, 10, 11, 18, 19*l*, 20
Shell 19*r*, 23
D.P. Wilson/Eric and David Hosking 24
Woodmansterne 29*r*
ZEFA 12*l*, 15, 17

EARTH SCIENCE LIBRARY

THE OCEANS

Contents

The blue planet

To an observer out in space our planet appears as a shining blue-white disk. Its color comes from the scattering of the Sun's light by the Earth's atmosphere and from the oceans that cover more than 70 percent of the surface.

Earth's brightness is due to its very high *albedo* – the reflecting power of its watery surface. Earth's albedo is 37 percent. That of the Moon, surprisingly, is only 7 percent.

For hundreds of years man could only study the oceans from sea level. Today, using special cameras in orbiting satellites, we can look down directly on to the swirling oceans and atmosphere that make Earth so different from other planets.

▽ The waters of the oceans and the water held in the atmosphere are all part of a never-ending cycle. Moisture is picked up by dry air as it moves across warm seas. Some condenses into cloud as it is carried along. Eventually, perhaps thousands of kilometers away, it will fall again as rain. Immediately the water starts to run downhill – in the rivers and streams that will carry it back to the sea again.

▷ A deep gash in the Earth's surface splits the bed of the Red Sea. Here, new rock is welling upward, steadily pushing North Africa and Saudi Arabia farther apart.

Pacific

Atlantic

Indian

△ The three major oceans as seen from space. The Pacific almost covers one hemisphere.

Roughly 200 million years ago the Earth's surface was very different from the familiar pattern of land and sea we know today. All the landmasses were grouped together into one vast supercontinent called Pangaea. The rest of the globe was covered by a single great ocean.

Slowly, the great landmass split apart. The pieces began to move over the Earth's surface, driven by slowly churning currents in the molten rocks beneath the Earth's hard, outer layers.

By about 35 million years ago the pattern of land and sea was very much like it is today. But the continents are still moving, and as the Atlantic and Indian oceans continue to get wider, by a few inches every year, the Pacific is slowly shrinking. At the northeast corner of Africa we can see the start of a new ocean. For the last 25 million years the Red Sea has been widening. If it continues at the same rate, in 200 million years it will be as wide as the Atlantic is today.

The riddle of the sea floor

Until the 1960s, earth scientists were faced with a difficult puzzle. Evidence had built up proving beyond a doubt that the continents had not always been in their present positions. The problem was that no one could explain *how* they had moved.

Detailed studies of the deep ocean floor in the 1960s revealed a huge mountain range, or ridge, winding through the central parts of the oceans. Further studies revealed deep grooves, or trenches, around the edges of many ocean basins.

Even more intriguing was the discovery that seabed rocks in the middle of the mountain ranges were very young, and that bands of rock at either side of the ridge became steadily older as the scientists moved outward from the ridge crest.

Finally, an exciting new theory emerged. It was called **plate tectonics**. We now believe that the Earth's **crust** and upper **mantle** are split into plates that float like rafts on semi-molten rocks below. The lighter rocks of the continents sit on these rafts and are carried along as they move.

▽ The diagram shows what we believe is happening beneath the Pacific Ocean.

Molten rock rises under the mid-ocean ridge, adding new rock to the sea bed. To the east, the moving sea-bed plate is forced down under the edge of the South American plate. The sea-bed rocks are melted, and **lava** is fed into the volcanoes of the Andes mountains. A deep trench marks where the plate plunges downward. In the west, similar sinking zones have produced the volcanic islands of Japan.

▽ The western Pacific has a complex system of volcanic island arcs (**1**) and sea-bed trenches (**2**). The greatest depth in any sea is in the Marianas Trench (see map).

Chains of islands (**3**) like those of Hawaii are formed over local "hot spots" in the crust.

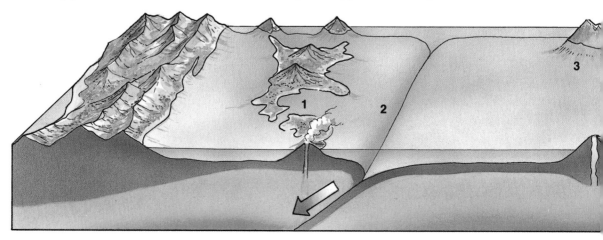

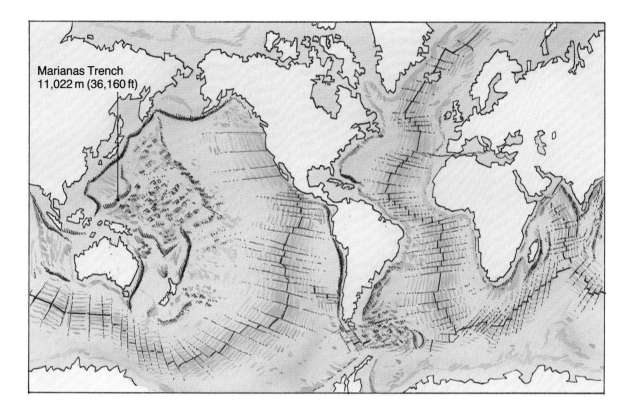

Marianas Trench
11,022 m (36,160 ft)

As for *how* they move, the theory is that currents in the semi-molten mantle are rising beneath the ocean ridges, spreading out, and then sinking again near the oceans' edges, carrying the continents with them.

△ If the world's oceans were drained, a fantastic landscape would be revealed – with mountains, valleys and gorges far more spectacular than any known on land.

▽ The mid-ocean ridge (**4**) has a deep central gash through which molten new rock rises.

The Andes (**5**) were formed by crumpling of the edge of the South American plate.

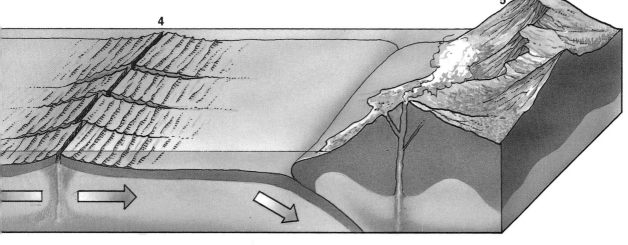

Ocean currents

Beyond the shoreline the sea bed slopes down very gently for some distance. Then, at a depth of about 140–180 m (450–600 ft) the slope steepens and the sea bed plunges to the deep ocean floor at about 3,660 m (12,000 ft). The shallow zone around the edge of the land is called the **continental shelf**.

Red flags and other danger signs displayed on some beaches warn of strong currents sweeping close to the shore. These are usually small but powerful local currents caused by the tides and waves that surge back and forth across the shallow continental shelf.

▽ Ocean currents carry plant and animal life from one place to another. Here, a drifting coconut has been washed ashore and has taken root. In this way even the bare lava of a new volcanic island may soon be covered in vegetation. Insects, too, may arrive on pieces of driftwood, while more seeds and insects arrive on the prevailing winds.

△ Icebergs are huge blocks of ice that have broken off **glaciers** pouring into the sea in the Arctic and Antarctic regions. Icebergs can drift for great distances, and one like this, from Greenland, sank the liner *Titanic* in 1912. It had been swept south into the path of the ship by the cold Labrador Current.

Warm currents

Cold currents

● Titanic sunk

△ The map shows the world's main ocean currents. In each ocean basin there is a roughly circular current flow called a *gyre*. The North Atlantic Gyre consists of the Equatorial Current, the Gulf Stream, the North Atlantic Current and the Canaries Current.

Out at sea it is a very different story. Here, far from the land's edge, the ocean waters are driven by two great wind systems. Close to the Equator the **Trade Winds** blow the surface waters westward. In the temperate zone, nearer the poles, the **Westerlies** blow the surface waters back toward the east. The result is that in each great ocean basin there is a roughly circular movement of the surface waters.

In the eastern parts of the oceans the currents are weak, often moving only 10 km (6 miles) in a day. But in the west the currents are stronger. The narrow Gulf Stream, for example, sweeps up the coast of North America and out into the Atlantic at up to 160 km (100 miles) a day.

Deep-water currents are very different. They consist of mainly of cold, heavy water spreading out into the ocean basins from the polar seas.

The scientist at sea

Oceanography, the scientific study of the seas and oceans, is a relatively young science.

During the 17th and 18th centuries the voyages of Captain James Cook and other great explorers produced the first accurate sea charts and the first attempts to measure ocean depths and currents, and the salinity, or saltiness, of the waters. Year by year human knowledge grew. In 1855 the American Matthew Fontaine Maury made the first charts of the Atlantic Ocean, and in 1872 the British government sent out the first truly scientific oceanographic expedition when HMS *Challenger* set sail on her four-year around-the-world voyage of research and discovery.

△ Many **submersibles** are specialized for scientific research. This one has a large observation window, lights and moveable arms.

▽ Ski-mounted sampling nets are towed over the sea bed to collect bottom-dwelling plants and animals.

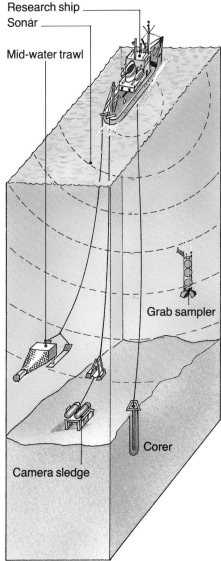

⊲ The instruments mounted inside this protective cage are used to measure the temperature and salinity of deep-water layers.

Research ship
Sonár
Mid-water trawl
Grab sampler
Corer
Camera sledge

Oceanographers today have specialized equipment to help them. Sampling nets can be towed along the sea bed or at any depth the scientist chooses. Grab samplers can be dropped to the sea bed to return with a "bite" of the bottom **sediments.** Corers go even deeper. Driven by weights and a suction system, their hollow tubes can penetrate 18 m (60 ft) into the sand and mud of the sea floor.

Electronic instrument packages can be sent into the depths to record pressure, temperature and salinity and to take water samples at various depths. And if photographs are wanted, cameras can be sent down on steerable powered "sleds," or the scientists themselves can venture into the deeps in a variety of submersibles.

Newest of all are the scientists' "electronic eyes" – the modern **sonar** (echo-sounding) systems that bounce sound waves off the sea bed and use the echoes to build up pictures of the shape and structure of the sea floor.

△ This diagram shows some of the techniques and equipment used by modern oceanographers to gather information about marine life and sea-bed sediments.

Explorers and traders

The first boats were simple rafts and dugout canoes. Yet even in such frail craft people ventured far out on the open oceans. We can only guess at their reasons. For some it was probably a need for more living space when homelands became crowded. For others it was perhaps a desire to trade, or simply to travel.

Whatever the reasons, incredible journeys were made in these simple craft. Nearly 40,000 years ago people crossed to Australia from Indonesia, almost certainly using only rafts. And between 5,000 and 2,000 years ago, waves of settlers from Asia spread throughout the islands of the Pacific, traveling in large canoes.

△ The oldest ship ever found is a river barge built for the Egyptian King Cheops 4,600 years ago. When Cheops died the ship was buried, in 1,224 pieces, close to his Great Pyramid at Gizeh.

△ **Outrigger** canoes, similar to these in Indonesia, have been used in the Pacific for several thousand years.

◁ A reconstruction of Drake's ship the *Golden Hind,* in which he became the first Englishman to sail around the world.

Five thousand years ago there was a brisk sea trade all around the shores of the Mediterranean Sea, but it was not until the 15th century that the great age of worldwide exploration began.

Between the 15th and 18th centuries the rapid development of the sailing ship and methods of navigation allowed European sailors to travel to the farthest corners of the globe. Empires grew up. Nations grew rich on the gold, silver and precious stones of other lands, and fortunes were made by those trading in spices and silk, tea, cotton and rare woods. The oceans had taken on a new importance. They had become worldwide highways for explorers and traders.

Today the world's sea lanes are crossed by highly specialized cargo vessels. Apart from a few luxury liners, passenger ships have now been replaced by air travel, but the seas remain the main highway for food products, raw materials, fuel oil and manufactured goods.

△ The Japanese tanker *Shin-Aitoku-Maru,* launched in 1980, combines ancient and modern technology.

Its fin-like sails work in exactly the same way as aircraft wings, producing a horizontal pulling force in place of the wing's vertical lift. A computer constantly adjusts the angle of the sail according to the wind direction, and automatically controls the combination of wind power and engine power for maximum efficiency.

The surging tides

If you spend a day by the sea, you are bound to notice the rise and fall of the tide. A longer stay would reveal something else. The tidal range – the difference between high and low tide – is constantly changing. Twice each month it reaches a maximum, and these large tides are called the **spring tides.** Halfway through the monthly cycle the range is much smaller, and these weak tides are called **neap tides.** What is not so obvious is that the tides are caused by the Moon.

Gravity is the force of attraction that always tries to pull two objects together. The Sun's huge gravitational force keeps the planets in their **orbits.** Earth's gravitational pull keeps us safely on the surface. The Moon, too, exerts a pull on the Earth. It has little effect on solid rock, but it does have a very great effect on the water of the Earth's oceans.

▽ The Sun and Moon both exert a pull on the oceans, but even though the Sun is 27 million times heavier than the Moon it is so far away that its pull is much weaker. However, it still has an effect on tides.

When Sun and Moon are in line, their gravitational pulls combine and produce the very big spring tides. When they are at right angles the pull is less and we get the much smaller neap tides.

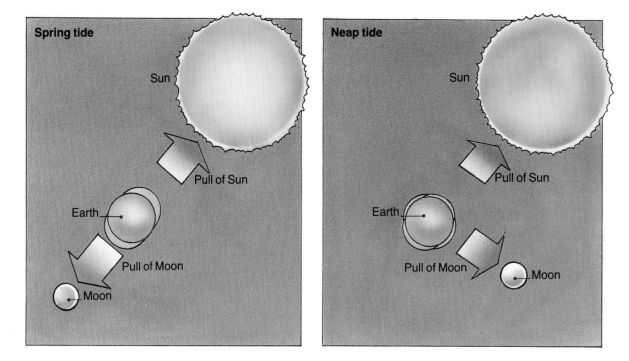

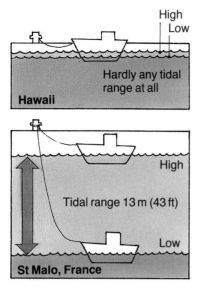

High
Low

Hawaii

Hardly any tidal range at all

High

Tidal range 13 m (43 ft)

Low

St Malo, France

△ Tidal ranges are usually small in mid-ocean but can be very large where tidal waters are funneled into a bay or river estuary.

▽ High tide completely surrounds Mont St. Michel in Brittany, France. Low tide exposes 16 km (10 miles) of sand. The tidal range here is 12.5 m (41 ft).

As the Moon travels around the Earth, it pulls the water on the nearest side of Earth outward into a bulge. A similar bulge on the opposite side of the Earth is caused by the water being thrown outward by the Earth's spin. These two bulges travel around the globe, producing the two high tides each day.

If the Earth were covered with water and the Moon's orbit were directly above the Equator, the tides would be the same all over the world. Unfortunately the story is not quite that simple. The oceans are trapped between odd-shaped landmasses, and their basins are broken up by mountain ranges. Even the Earth's spin affects the way the water moves as it sloshes about.

The result is that tides can vary enormously from place to place. And because the Moon's orbit carries it a long way north and south of the Equator, its pull is lopsided, making one of the daily high tides bigger than the other.

Wind waves and tsunamis

Wind-driven storm waves can crash into the coast with enormous force. During a storm in the English Channel, for example, a 65-ton block of concrete was wrenched from a breakwater at Cherbourg in northern France and hurled 18 m (60 ft) up the beach.

Waves start off as tiny ripples caused by the wind blowing over the water. As these ripples grow into small waves, the effect of the wind is magnified. As well as pushing against the upwind side of the wave, the wind swirls into an eddy on the downwind side, reducing the pressure there and making it easier for the wave to move.

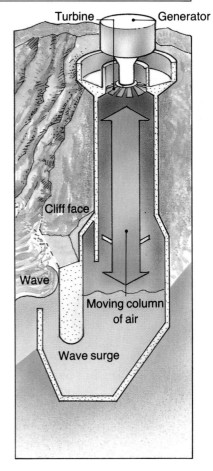

Turbine — Generator

Cliff face

Wave

Moving column of air

Wave surge

△ This new installation in Norway uses wave power to generate electricity.

As each wave hits the coast it pushes a surge of water up the concrete tower. This in turn pushes air in the tower through a turbine at the top. The turbine blades continue to spin as air rushes back between waves, and electricity is generated continuously.

◁ Waves offer a constant supply of power – if man's technology can harness them.

Just how big a wave grows depends on three things: the strength of the wind, the length of time the wind blows, and the fetch – that is, the distance over which the wind is blowing. Waves of 50 feet (15 m) are an impressive sight, but the biggest sea wave ever recorded was one of 112 feet (34 m) in the Pacific in 1933.

Once the wind drops, or the waves pass out of the storm area, the waves change shape. From ragged, sharp-peaked storm waves they settle into gentler, more rounded swell waves that can travel for thousands of miles across the sea.

The biggest waves of all are often wrongly called tidal waves. Their proper name is **tsunami**, a Japanese word. They are caused not by tides but by earthquakes or volcanic eruptions on or under the seabed. Far out at sea, tsunamis are not impressive. The crests of the waves may be only 3 feet (1 m) high, while the distance between the crests may be 95 miles (150 km). Tsunamis can travel at 500 mph (800 km/h). When they reach shallow coastal waters, they can rear up to 130 feet (40 m), causing enormous damage to coastal areas.

△ Every surfer's dream. A huge Pacific breaker curls over to form an almost perfect tube of clear water.

Surfing is popular in many parts of the world, but Hawaii, the coast of California and the east coast of Australia are famous for their waves.

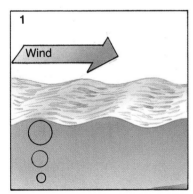

1 Once clear of the storm area, waves settle into gentle rounded swell waves. Water particles inside the wave have a circular motion.

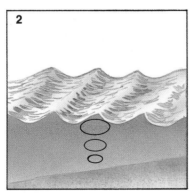

2 As the wave runs into shallower water, the circular paths of the water particles are compressed and the wave starts to rear up.

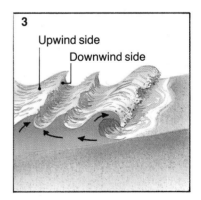

3 Finally, as it nears the beach, the wave becomes unstable. It topples over and spills forward. This kind of wave is called a breaker.

Exploring the deep

The first successful piece of diving equipment was invented in 1690 by Edmund Halley. It was a bell-shaped vessel, open at the bottom but with air trapped in the upper part. The air supply was topped up from weighted air-filled barrels.

Helmeted diving suits fed by air pumped through a pipe from the surface came into use in the 1830s. This traditional type of "hard hat" suit has remained in use, with very few changes, right up to the present day. It is, however, only used in relatively shallow water.

The breakthrough in undersea exploration came in 1943 when Jacques Cousteau and Emile Gagnan tested their Self-Contained Underwater Breathing Apparatus (SCUBA). This equipment did away with air pipes and heavy clothing. The diver could swim freely, using flippers and taking air from cylinders carried on the back.

△ Scuba equipment is ideal for diving in shallow waters. For deeper work, especially for heavy work in the cold dark waters of harbors and docks, tough protective "hard hat" suits are worn.

Since 1943, diving equipment has greatly improved. Different mixtures of gases are now used, depending on the depth of the dive. Air can be used safely as far down as about 60 m (200 ft) but at greater depths a mixture of oxygen and **helium** is breathed.

The search for oil in recent years has brought about great advances in undersea technology. Divers now operate from anchored **habitats** – resting and eating in these pressurized underwater "houses" between dives, and often staying underwater for long periods. For very deep work, submersibles are used. These small, highly specialized diving vessels can tackle a huge range of tasks. Some are manned; some are operated by remote control. They are equipped with lights, cameras, manipulator arms and even with underwater cutting and welding equipment.

▽ The JIM suit is part-way between a diving suit and a small submersible. It is made of aluminum alloy to withstand great pressure. The diver, working inside at normal air pressure, can descend to depths of 460 m (1,500 ft).

◁ A commercial submersible being lifted from the waters of the North Sea after a reconnaissance dive. Such vessels are used for finding lost equipment, planning routes for pipelines, inspecting underwater installations and carrying out repairs and maintenance work.

19

History on the sea bed

◁ The cleared interior of a wrecked merchant ship found near Kyrenia, Cyprus. The ship, loaded with amphorae (wine jars), sank at the time of Alexander the Great.

△ Objects recovered from the wreck of the *Association* included clay pipes, part of a bugle, a clasp, part of a spoon and a broken bottle, still corked. *Association* sank 300 years ago off the Scilly Isles off southwest Britain.

Imagine the hundreds of thousands of ships that have traveled the world's oceans through the ages. Imagine, too, the thousands that have perished – swamped by tropical hurricanes, dashed to pieces on jagged reefs, or sunk in sea battles.

When a ship goes down, it is not only the hull and masts that plunge to the sea bed. With them also go the ship's cargo and food, its charts and navigation instruments; the clothing, weapons, plates and spoons of the officers and crew – even their personal belongings, including the clay pipes, dice and musical instruments with which they passed their spare time.

Each wreck is a time capsule – a perfectly preserved fragment of seafaring history.

The invention of scuba equipment – the **aqualung** – has brought hundreds of these time capsules within reach of underwater archaeologists.

Exploring a wreck is a slow process. The whole area must be surveyed and its currents studied. Seldom does a wreck lie all in one piece. Its timbers and contents may be scattered over a wide area. The site is always marked out with a grid of scaffolding or tapes so that the exact position of every timber and object can be recorded.

And even when the ship's contents have been brought up, the task has barely started. Objects that have been in water for hundreds of years are fragile. They must be painstakingly preserved before they can be placed on display.

△ *Wasa* was a three-masted warship built in Sweden in 1628. She was 70 m (230 ft) long and 12 m (39 ft) broad, and carried 64 guns. Sadly, her design was top-heavy. Barely a sea-mile from where she was launched, she overturned and sank in 35 m (115 ft) of water in Stockholm harbor. The hull was raised, almost intact, in 1959 but the detailed restoration work lasted until the late 70s.

Minerals from the sea

Sea water contains well over 80 different chemical substances. Some are dissolved in the water, others drift about as tiny particles. The most common chemicals are sodium and chloride, combined as salt. In some parts of the world salt is still extracted from sea water by methods that have been used for thousands of years. Most of the other chemicals are found in such minute quantities that they are not worth extracting.

Many valuable mineral deposits are found in the shallow waters of the continental shelf. Most of these came originally from land. As the rocks containing them were worn away and washed into the sea, particles of heavy minerals such as iron, tin and gold would settled on the sea bed, often very close to the shore. These are called "placer deposits" and are usually worked by bucket dredgers or suction equipment.

▽ In warm regions, salt is easily extracted from sea water by the natural process of evaporation. Here in Lebanon, windmills are used to pump sea water into shallow pans. The water evaporates in the hot sun, leaving behind a layer of salt crystals.

△ Much of the world's tin is extracted by bucket dredgers from the sandbanks of the shallow coastal waters of Thailand and Indonesia.

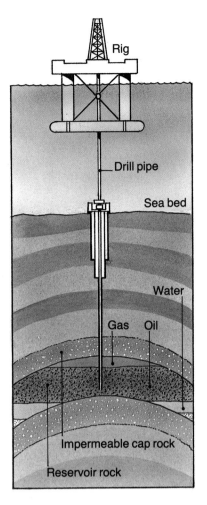

Rig

Drill pipe

Sea bed

Water

Gas Oil

Impermeable cap rock

Reservoir rock

In recent years a new mineral wealth has been found in the rock layers deep beneath the sea-bed mud of the continental shelf. The great prizes here have been oil and natural gas. Several different geological structures can trap these valuable minerals but the most common is the **anticline** – an arched rock formation. The oil and gas are held in the tiny spaces between the grains of a **reservoir rock** such as sandstone. An overlying layer of **impermeable** rock, such as clay, prevents the oil or gas from escaping and seeping upward to the sea bed.

Unusual mineral deposits have also been discovered on the deep sea floor. They consist of nodules – rounded lumps about the size of tennis balls. They are made mainly of manganese and iron, but also contain copper, nickel and cobalt. Nodules may perhaps provide a mineral resource for the future, but at present it would be too costly to try to raise them.

△ To reach an oil or gas field it is sometimes necessary to drill through several thousand meters of rock. For the hardest rocks, diamond-tipped drill-bits must be used.

The diagram shows the structure of an anticline oil-trap. There is always some gas trapped along with the oil. Most of it is piped ashore but for safety reasons some has to be flared off.

▷ Oil-production platforms in the North Sea's Brent oil-field with flare stacks burning.

Life in the oceans

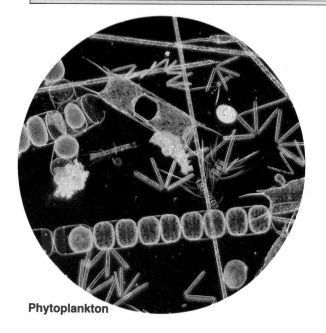

Phytoplankton

Zooplankton

The most important form of life in the oceans is so small we can see it only through a microscope. It is called **plankton** and consists of billions of minute plants called phytoplankton and tiny animals, not much bigger, called zooplankton.

The phytoplankton drift in the warm surface waters of the oceans and perform the same vital role as grasses, trees and other plants on land. They "fix" the energy of the Sun and use it to build new plant cells. The zooplankton feed on the phytoplankton – and then in turn provide the main source of food for slightly larger animals.

One way or another, all marine animals depend on plankton. Many different kinds of shellfish, for example, live on plankton which they filter out of the water. The shellfish may then be eaten by a seal, which in turn may fall prey to a killer whale. Biologists call this succession of who-eats-whom a **food chain.** Each one starts with plankton and ends with a top predator like a whale or shark.

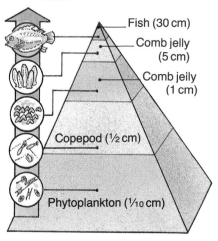

Fish (30 cm)
Comb jelly (5 cm)
Comb jelly (1 cm)
Copepod (½ cm)
Phytoplankton (¹⁄₁₀ cm)

△ The pyramid shows how food energy is passed up a food chain. It takes millions of phytoplankton to feed one zooplankton; perhaps 100,000 zooplankton to feed a small comb jelly; several thousand small comb jellies to feed one big one, and perhaps a dozen large comb jellies to feed the fish at the top.

Sunlight

◁ By far the most crowded zone of the sea is the top 200 m (650 ft). Here, light can penetrate the waters, which are rich in drifting phytoplankton.

The zooplankton, the next link in the food chain, consist mainly of the **larvae** of other creatures – everything from fishes to whelks and crabs, jellyfish and sea urchins.

As depth increases, the number of animals becomes less and less. At very great depths, animal life is very sparse. Many deep-sea fishes have their own glowing lights to help them find food and a mate in the total darkness of the deeps.

Even in the clearest waters the Sun's rays are filtered out at about 200 m (650 ft). Below that lies a twilight zone inhabited by lantern fish, squid and deep-diving hunters like the sperm whale. Deeper still, and the inky blackness is home to some of the strangest sea creatures of all, including gulper eels with elastic stomachs and angler fish with glowing lights to lure their prey within range.

Lighted zone	Surface 650 feet
Twilight zone	3,300 feet
Dark zone	20,000 feet
Deepest trench	37,000 feet

△ This diagram shows the lighted zone, the twilight zone and the dark zone to scale. Deeper still lie the oceanic trenches.

The ocean wanderers

In winter each year tourists and scientists gather on the shores of the Gulf of California to watch the arrival of the magnificent gray whales at the southern end of their annual **migration**. The whales spend the summer in the Arctic Ocean and North Pacific, feeding on plankton and small fish. In November and December they travel south so that the females can give birth in the warm waters off California and Mexico. The whales mate again soon after the calves are born, and in spring they head north again to their Arctic feeding grounds.

The migration of the gray whale involves a round trip of about 10,000 km (6,200 miles) and is just one of the many remarkable journeys made each year by sea mammals, seabirds and fish.

▷ Short-tailed shearwaters (called muttonbirds in New Zealand and Australia) migrate from their breeding grounds to the Arctic every year. The bird's curious figure-eight course (shown below) enables it to use the prevailing winds, and also carries it over areas where food will be in good supply.

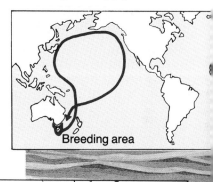

Breeding area

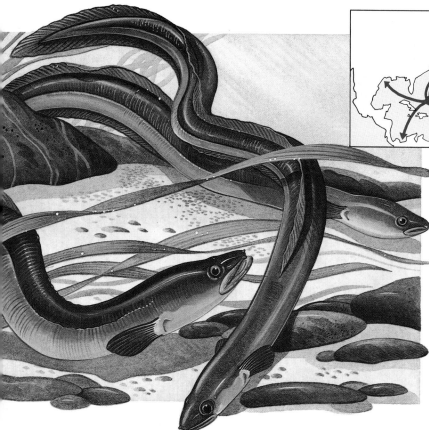

Breeding area
➡N. American eels
➡European eels

△ The eels that are found in the freshwater rivers of Europe and North America are **spawned** in the Sargasso Sea – an area of the western Atlantic noted for its calm waters and masses of floating weed. The eel larvae are carried north by the Gulf Stream Current. They grow to maturity in freshwater rivers and lakes, then return to the Sargasso Sea to spawn – and to die.

Pacific and Atlantic salmon hatch far inland in freshwater streams, but spend most of their adult life at sea. As long as eight years later they return to breed, using an almost unbelievably sensitive sense of smell to guide them back to the very same streams in which they were born.

The greatest long-distance migrants of all, however, are the seabirds. The Arctic tern spends half the year in the Arctic, half in the southern oceans bordering Antarctica – a round trip of 40,000 km (25,000 miles) that involves almost eight months of nonstop flying. The short-tailed shearwater comes a close second, traveling 32,000 km (20,000 miles) each year over the Pacific.

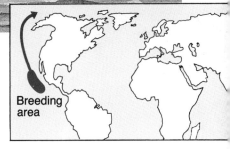

Breeding area

△ Large groups of the California gray whale enter the warm calm waters of the Gulf of California during their breeding season. The whales often raise their huge bodies right out of the water as if taking a good look around. The California gray was almost hunted out of existence, but is now protected by law.

Food from the sea

Hundreds of different fishing methods are used around the world. One of the most common is the surrounding net. This is a long narrow net run out from the beach by people wading or paddling canoes. It is carried out in a wide arc and then brought back to the beach where it is hauled ashore by the people of the village.

Weighted lines are trailed on the sea bed to catch bottom-dwelling fish. Long lines with baited hooks are used for fast hunters like tuna.

Fish are also caught with fish-traps and entangling nets, baskets and spears. There is no end to the traditional fisherman's ingenuity.

▽ These boats have worked together as a team, using their nets to surround a big shoal of fish. The fish are now being hoisted aboard the fishing boats with large scoop-nets suspended from the boats' derricks and operated by powerful winches.

◁ Fish-traps off the coast of Sri Lanka. The long walls of netting supported on poles will guide the fish into the high-walled fish-traps. Note the egrets and cormorants hanging around for an easy meal!

Modern deep-sea fishing, by contrast, is a highly mechanized industry. The two main methods are purse-seining and trawling.

Purse-seines are very big surrounding nets operated by fast, powerful boats. They are used in the warm waters of the Atlantic, Pacific and Indian oceans, usually for catching tuna. These nets can surround a whole school of fish, and the boats can hold up to 1,500 tons of frozen fish in their holds.

Even bigger are the modern factory trawlers. These ships locate their prey with echo-sounding equipment. The enormous bag-shaped trawl net is then towed through the shoal and hauled in up a ramp in the ship's stern. The whole catch is processed immediately, on board, and is delivered to port boxed and frozen.

Unfortunately our knowledge of fish migration routes and the efficiency of modern catching methods have resulted in the overfishing of many traditional fishing grounds.

△ Fish is an important source of animal protein food in many parts of the world. Here, sun-dried fish is offered for sale in a local market in Mali, West Africa.

Glossary

Anticline An arched rock formation caused by crumpling of the rock layers. A similar shallow U-shaped formation is called a syncline. The two types are often found together where rock layers have been crushed and squeezed.

Aqualung A trade name for one kind of portable under-water breathing apparatus.

Continental shelf The outer edge of the continent, which lies under the sea. The shelf averages 80–240 km (50–150 miles) wide and its outer edge is usually at a depth of about 180 m (600 ft).

Crust The outer solid skin of

the Earth. Under the oceans the crust is only about 6 km (3½ miles) thick. Continental crust is much thicker at up to 35 km (22 miles) but may reach 70 km (44 miles) beneath high mountain ranges.

Food chain A series of animals, in which each species depends on the next one along for its main source of food. A common example from your garden might be cat-bird-spider-fly.

Glacier A moving river of ice that flows down a mountain under its own weight. Glaciers carve their own valleys, much deeper and wider than those carved by rivers.

Habitat To a biologist, a habitat is the natural home of a plant or animal, such as a woodland habitat, a marine habitat and so on.

To divers, a habitat is an underwater base in which they can rest, eat and sleep without returning to the surface.

Helium An invisible odorless gas used in aqualungs for dives below 60 m (200 ft). Air is a mixture of oxygen and nitrogen, but nitrogen causes problems such as the "bends." For diving purposes the nitrogen is replaced by helium which is less troublesome.

Impermeable Something which will not allow gas or liquid

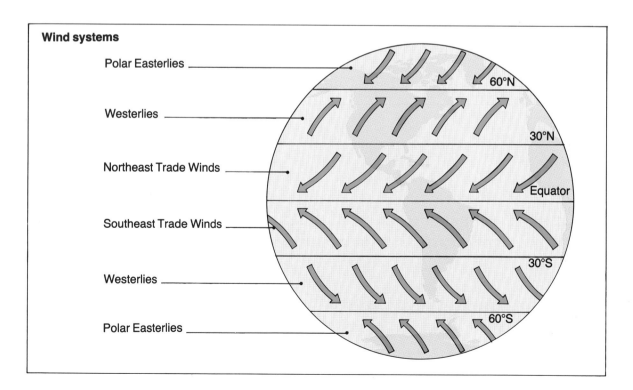

Wind systems

Polar Easterlies

Westerlies

Northeast Trade Winds

Southeast Trade Winds

Westerlies

Polar Easterlies

60°N

30°N

Equator

30°S

60°S

to pass through. Impermeable rocks trap oil and gas in deep rock layers, preventing them from seeping to the surface.

Larva (plural, larvae) The form some animals take between hatching out of the egg and finally becoming adults. Often the larval stage looks nothing at all like the animal's final adult form.

Lava The name given to molten rock poured out on to the Earth's surface during a volcanic eruption.

Mantle The layer of the Earth's interior immediately beneath the crust. It is about 2,900 km (1,800 miles) thick and is part-solid, part-molten.

Migration The regular movement of an animal from one place to another.

Neap tides The small-range tides that occur when the Sun's gravitational pull and the Moon's gravitational pull are not reinforcing each other.

Oceanography The scientific study of the seas and oceans.

Orbit The circular or elliptical path taken around the Sun by the planets, or the path taken around the Earth by the Moon or a satellite.

Outrigger A long piece of wood or an extra float held out on poles from the side of a canoe to give it greater stability. Outrigger canoes are typical of the Pacific region.

Plankton Tiny animals and plants that drift in the surface waters of the oceans.

Plate tectonics The study of the movements of the large plates that make up the Earth's surface.

Reservoir rock Any kind of rock that can hold oil, gas or water. The rock acts rather like a sponge, storing the gas or liquid in tiny spaces between its grains.

Sediments Sand, silt, mud or the remains of small marine animals that have sunk to the sea bed. After millions of years, these soft substances are turned into solid rocks such as sandstone, mudstone and chalk.

Sonar A system of detecting objects under water, or of gaining a picture of the shape of the sea bed, using sound waves and their reflections. The word comes from **so**und **na**vigation and **r**anging.

Spawned Means "produced in the form of eggs." When fish lay their eggs they are said to be spawning.

Spring tides The large tides produced twice each month when the Sun and Moon are in line so that their gravitational pulls are combined.

Submersible Any craft that can be taken under water. The word is used for small research and commercial vessels rather than large submarines.

Trade Winds A broad band of winds at either side of the Equator. The Northeast Trade Winds carried the first seafarers to the New World. They were named because of their importance to merchant ships in the age of sail.

Tsunami A large wave caused by an earthquake or volcanic eruption in the rocks beneath the ocean bed.

Westerlies Bands of winds lying outside the Trade Winds, that is, nearer the poles. It was these winds that carried sailing ships back to Europe from the Americas.

Index

PRINTED IN BELGIUM BY

proost
INTERNATIONAL BOOK PRODUCTION